How You'll Work Your Way to Me

The Memoir

Xanh Lửa

Audio Reccomended

For Me and Only Me

the ending was mid

a climax is a soft deadline and a stupid end

welcome to part 2.

pattern recognition

started writing this on
02/22/2024

222 a sunrise
summed up 6

2024
8

the prior written on 01/23 2024

123 dusk

together
6

6 & 6
quick math

12

military time

0

where it all began

from nothing.

a return to origins

origins are arbitrary

the first book was one

origins are important.

it was the car ride to lowell

voice memos

the book was originally about self discovery

a for you mirror and a mirror for you

both selfishly

were just

for me

f(everything)

everything is contrived she said,
i ended up saying, and you never said

or i never heard

for you and only you is a voyeuristic lie

well kind of

for me and only me is a voyeuristic truth

it's certain

4 sets of twins inside of me
a gemini stellium i initially didn't see

multiplied by the libra who can hold 2 truths

then turned to its side

an even simpler equation

it was me all along.

things are adding up

04/07/2002

all together 15
combined is 6

the lovers you are

05/18/2002

added together is 18
added again is 9

the hermit I am

still polar opposites
but you were right

i needed to spend more time

alone without you

for me and only me

it will be soon after you read this

maybe in this life or the next

you'll realize the first was a decoy

and that the first before that at co works with
two banana milks and an I'm sorry
letter you never read
was a decoy as well

third times is maybe a charm

not a guaruntee but a plea to the universe for luck

a request for a platonic love that once was,

with a made clear romantic intention
for the future

but in the spaces in between a once was and
a future that may never be

is time to make patient memory once again

a humble request
to skate down mutual benefit

a butter knife

the money from this. all of this.

a ride in Mars like usual

you asked for a cut not a whole

i inversed— gave you a whole not a cut

mirror twice and return to origins

10, 20?

in the middle
15

a percentage of me you get now defined

an investment friend I said you were

mirror

actually it was me with a 10% ROI

150— the first parking fine for Mars you helped me with.

quick math

divide

$15 per book

an even price

15% of an infinite money
generator
made during winter

a plan still intact
made during summer

my first promise said to you

never broken

and a second one
                    comes soon

what happens when the sun finally sees herself?

what becomes of her reflection,
is it melted
recreated

does she learn to feel her own radiance

or does she turn and flee from fire to inevitably face herself
realizing she needs to stand firm, hold tight and burn
brighter.

does she break the rules and stare at herself?

looking at every pore and every solar flare.

does she kiss herself then? because
what else is there to do.

Does she witness her own supernova

then worship her own heat running her fingers
across the surface of her skin

does she realize she's everything ever

then does she masturbate

licking her own flame

and indulging in the origins of the universe

before once again seeing herself

and coming full circle.

things i'll admit at sunrise

you walk and walked so i can and could run.

that's actually a lie i learned to walk my self and you did too

i got two motherfuckin legs for a reason

not even sunrise anymore 1:47am

hours after slam free or die

died on the first round
and I'm free once again

slams are arbitrary
open mics are where religions are made

an ode to self worship

hyper independence is a safety net
a lifestyle called self trust

belief in myself
intuition internalized

mean more to myself than words can even fathom

then fathom the words to make myself more meaningful

an afterthought of a phantom
and a ghost of a shell

echoes of a myself orgy

our limited boundary
my infinite one

a magic self mirror
called alone time

mercury entering pisces
fuel to the imagination

moon in leo
inside and out

inverse square law

light dither
specular reflection

the study of light science to see myself
schoolism

references only we get
your green singing bowl
mine blue

sounds touching sacral
the sweet little lady I am

news flash
gender reveal:
everything

only they & sometimes them
keep me at the beginning of sentences

pay respects to me at the end.

self criticality a skill
self love an instinct

an invitation to my world

voyeurism
view me fuck myself silly

shameless indulgence in island skin
lunar calendar on my sleeve
moving at a snails pace
slow is fast, fast is slow

mirrored
i said keep up at the woodshop
slow down

separate function from linguistic veneer

listen to what i'm doing and see what I'm saying
book one horrifying book two a light
welcome home to seeing yourself

yet again

phantom

The first song in a playlist you made me in late spring

ghost;

an introduction to Math rock,

of a poetry collection about a brother no longer

the scent of a phantom found in a land of ice, early winter

agential in my own self ornamentation
somewhere between east and south east

you'll find the south where you're from and the
place i happened to find myself in

a vietnamese nail tech confusing me for japanese or korean

a then return to my northern home

the mochinut you've never been inside by the haffner's we
momentarily stopped at

i walk in

a plum wintermelon tea light on the ice and sugar

the lady there, Vietnamese, sees me past an east asian
veneer

and says con

double infinity found in a walmart

single ply 88 sheet paper towel roll from the lucky green
walmart in north carolina

a selfie taken 4 weeks later on the 23rd of break up month

one month exactly since the first and a timeline to be
corrected in the soon second

mini feedback loops
grandiosity not appealing

chaos theory,
    always a question of what's next

suspense is an effortless venture
keep you on your toes
break the 5th wall

take you down a notch
 4 walls one home

stick to it

gotchu in a perfect square
find the root

  2

create the binary again
rewind time
an imaginary number
negative that shit
create the shadowrealm

chart a journey
break it off at the asymptote

destroy y=mx+b

no slopes only gains
create the S curve
logistic growth
cap population density

control how people see the world
related rates
speed of a shadow

derive with respect to time
derived myself over and over
find C

a constant absolute truth
add to the position function
change the location

derive for velocity
amp it up
absolute value
two walls side by side

fast is slow and slow is fast
speed it up
unintentionally miscalc
then name it a detour down memory lane

control the speed with respect to time
derive again
accelerate

gotta go fast so slow the fuck down
meditate
listen to rain sounds
sleep with a clean conscience
pray to change itself

wake up
find the lim(x) as I approach infinity

break the lim
continuity
effortless flow

ti-84 deluxe
an MIT kid's wet dream
my reality

gender pokemon
mathematical incelism plus
masc lesbian abg

no games on my phone
can't stop won't stop grind
shiny hunting for the you
twitch stream of consciousness
the AP lang mindset
check me out in hiking gear
salomon XA-alpine 2s

going on a journey
redefining home in my body

pitstop at the intersection between
language and math

invent a field of study
analyze every sign
contrive a romance

inflate platonic love
milk existence

find a true name
end at a multidimensional climax
mirror the book

derive even further
reverse outline to poetry

inverse the cover
zoom in pixellate
zoom out the structure

layer that shit
put both side by side
yin and yang butterfly

origins of the universe and mathematical intentions behind
found in the moments when
two books finally meet each other in
the palm of your hands for

the first time.

you and me at 3:28

this title is a lie it's 8:46

now 9:44

wrote 18 poems yesterday

number unfathomable
the righteous unbelieved

a godlike normalcy
an average sapphic reality

take back what I said
shove it right back

lesbianism wins
dial it up to the queers
derive it

language itself
lit on fire
flow state

entrepreneurial self help
atomic habits of being god everyday

tech bro architecture
sucking my own dick

make him ethereal
turn him to a yona
inverse the gender laws
he's now a she

self critique of an imaginary sex scene found

between two dashes that highlight actual intentionality

an ever expanding platonic love
looking to be besties 4ever

a kiss is a meteor shower waiting to happen

a hand hold tsunami starter

avatar the last airbender
aang and zuko fanfic

todoroki comes

best mashup of the century

Dabi is born

two faced BlueFlare
a minecraft username

an animated your name plotline
body switch enmeshment
cross referencing every movie we watched
split and spliced every trope

then weave it together as one
throw it up
magical superpower

life is a movie
get high again
set a boundary
break it
repair the 4th wall
jump to the 6th
skip to the 7th

blow up the imagination
allegory
promised neverland season 3
repairing the trainwreck of season 2

third times a charm not a guarantee

intentional self repetition spaced apart
between the universes
of filled pages

break genre and classification itself
a sci-fi breaking memoir and
a mathematic literary analysis poetry collection

double triple quad entendre
using words I heard yesterday

a flow that touches every poet's heart

then suddenly
a destruction of their minds

literary ejaculation

mentality blown repaired again shattering continuity
what is there to even say

but watch pretty colors unfold
an old instagram name

connections made so loosely
gripped only by sound itself

speed of images moving
graphic analysis

slow down

breathe

just kidding stole your breath away
took away the spacing
literary genius

skip the 8th
nevermind
9th wall
reveal the 10th but keep it mysterious

I'm in your head actively writing the universe

warping your sense
 of space and time

that memory 3 years ago

now come back here

you saw it— and i didn't
but i made you see
welcome to a mind fuck
a brain orgy
sponging your fucking head

flow of the universe
tongue twister
screwed up

tea bag
gg

now go suck your dick
twisting the your

grow a pair
make it two
top and bottom
make it switch

gender analysis
double infinity

make them meet
rupture of the self
body in a pretzel

breathe out an undo button
wring out the body rag

slow down the images
let the audience breathe damn

add in a damn for punchline

throw in a lastly to cut the flow

and lastly,

give them a pat on the head for surviving
an existentialist nightmare

and an artificial heart attack.

a start before groceries 15:16

A new origin point

ran my fingertips through my hair
A fresh shower

arbitrary to do lists
named self care and what sounds yummy

I don't mind pants today
time skip 6:22 setting up the google doc
bouncing between one medium and another
both digital

and suddenly
a swift end to this poem providing lyrical shortness to
contrast the density of the last poem

and serving as a brief intermission for

the collection of platonic love poems upcoming

from you to me

I saw everything except how I'm
going to greet you
or you greet me

there's a zone between the knowledge of god and
mortalisms called

fucking certain uncertainty

an uncomfortably comfortable space of both knowing and
forgetting
at the same time.

I'm fucking with the you
yes you but not

you

mirroring the clarity of hieroglyphic analysis with

tonal ambiguity
me and you
you and me

you have no fucking clue when I'm addressing you anymore
and you're grasping to the tonality of a bible with redacted
sentences and

stories not actually told.

you're realizing

that chaos theory is a masterclass in learning how
to go with the flow

moments of us that linger still and always

Me catching up to you in wynncraft

sitting by mem hall people watching with the
$20 avocado toast you bought me from bolt

your second attempt at agedashi tofu

the facetime call in warby parker

Alara being jealous of your pants that one day at the wood
shop.

you always saying Alora instead of Alara

getting my septum pierced post break up
with what felt like
you by my side

watching you get your momentary eyebrow piercing

you coming home after getting your first tattoo

you making fun of me because you have better
form on the table saw

you telling me not to laugh
me holding back laughter then laughing later

your once empty apartment, built like a bad minecraft
house.

our trip to the antique mall that day

me fueling your ongoing salami turned to prosciutto
addiction

you hitting your first ollie and texting me about it

outings for sparkling orange dry from east side marketplace

you forgiving me for the shittiest undercut I gave you

the day in the met roasting people in Vietnamese

us with our headphones on
music loud
6ft apart
silently cruising down the east side bike path

And every single time we've noticed something
cũng được worthy, turned to each other,
and giggled.

to you from me

linguistic self mutilation
undead unluck

actualities of a self serenade
glistening grunge
a to self referential

lust and indignance
missed trajectories

multiplicities of none
activated by abstract complexities

chewing words
bodily spit

sisyphus is a cool sound and a memory forgotten

My body is a bellona shrine disguised as a buddhist sanctuary

loose terminologies for wars frozen in the thick of things

words that carry meaning only in a once digested head
image

poetry is my fucking ejaculate

method acting is a reality

everything is an arbitrary denominator and
categorical grouping for an amount not
linguistic quantifiable given a limited amount of time

everywhere is a spatial generalism that is not commonly
used and most notably seen as a relational that groups an
unfathomable amount of spatial zones into hieroglyphic
digestibility

and all at once is how

everything

everywhere

happened.

playing with words; lyrics about wordplay— finding a home in every sentence

Please undo me

ungender
unname
unfind me

unrealize everything
hit the undo button over and over again only to find me in the spaces between sentences and paragraphs

and the gaps in between words and periods.

remember that gap

that moment right before things truly end and you move on, you always have the option to undo time itself

another chance

an olive branch is a romance and a reset is a eulogy

i hope you believe in paying respect to the dead

so please as a final request before the sentence ends

and a black hole called a period makes it's appearance

set up a dash, a comma, anything of the moment to buy some time

keep the flow continuing,

keep playing with the
sentence

the structure

the space in between line breaks

trust your use of language

strike through the unnecessary

delete delete delete

bolden yourself

italicize the exotic

underline the epic

now step back unwind

page blank no longer

map of your mind

heart and soul plastered about

spliced up and put back together

then hit the redo button. break all the rules

now watch everything disappear

flip everything upside down

clear the page

room for opportunity

words become sand

and quick before they all come again and
you're drowning 7 pages deep in a paper
you don't care about

essence that shit

reverse outline

inverse the structure

remap every sentence

add in a lyric

dedicate it to the love of your life

put it in the footnotes

throw MLA in the trash
Light APA on fire

throw in two column notes if you want to

let yourself breathe through every sentence

tear through every paragraph

unapologize your writing

unsorry yourself

destroy formalities

stick to music

start a codependent relationship with the universe

break everything up

nothing makes sense again

cite a theory of pure chaos

drop the paper

fake a family emergency
take a damn break
walk outside

hit up a boba shop

get a fucking crepe

healthy relationship with the self

take two laps around

come back in a circle

then split it apart

just make sure shit sounds nice

revisit the google drive

delete the paper

turn in a sticky note with a drawing of a middle finger

call it performance art

fuck with the professor's mind

tell them to sit the fuck down and get a better degree

make themselves useful in a world too short too long and
too moving for
antiqued unchanging formats

tell them academia is flacid

has erectile dysfunction

and can fuck itself with its broken condom

then tell them to suck their format

learn to have sex with their own damn words

pick up an instrument

love language itself

rekindle an old passion

use everything as a mirror reflection to see how beautiful
they are

how beautiful life is and can be

so they can finally stand up walk outside of
the classroom enlightened

smell a damn flower

drink a good coffee

and breathe in a world where rules can be shattered
completely

pieced back together

and undone once again

to find an everlasting solace in the breathing room between
the last words of a sentence and the periods that start

new worlds.

if you shall return

remember to take care of you first

yes,

you

take your time and take plenty

any time and all time

remember to grab your fanny pack and
your lunar phase skateboard

remember to slow down and see yourself in a mirror

know you're funnier than you believe, smarter than you
think, and capable of anything on your own

then when ready
come see me as any you

and know

when or if you come searching

though I'm mine and only mine
you'll always find me truly yours

memories I recently found breathing again

at the home depot in mars
you said the rain would clear
i said it would keep on raining

it was both

a dorm room fire not started but almost

a first but not first date at pho horn

a shared value for pure pho broth

later the ceiling at pho saigon

the apartment on hope st you only briefly had
before i stole you for a summer

your mother's voice at T.F. Green

the container store in cranston
nước mắm in my talenti container
your balcony facing a once was
your final net not hanging there

and us plant shopping at the Jordan's jungle

all the me's you've yet to meet

the me that learned to smile
who tenderly caresses every mirror reflection treating her
like a blessing from the universe

the me who has learned to laugh more
who let's their body fall to the ground vulnerable,
not afraid of the speed of their knees dropping,

their stomach buckling

and the ever increasing volume of their laughter's echo

the me who sings to themselves
serenading the universe with the sound of a planet and
comet kissing,
two stars shooting across

and the voice of a butterfly screaming it's own name

the me that writes myself love poems giving care to every
child inside of this body
becoming an evergrowing ancestor for me's yet to be

the me that explores themselves
climbing outside of internal dungeons,
escaping shadows that once were
by taking the long way round seeing every nook and cranny,
every hole in the wall,
remembering
to not miss any gorgeous spots

the me that praises icarus for finally reaching the sun. they
never had to fly, wings scorched.
simply needed to look down
and see their ocean reflection.

the me that fully loves kevin.
Who tenderly holds that child, taking him on adventures
he's never been on, giving him an older sister he's always
wanted and turning a big scary world into a bite-sized day-
dream

the me that makes everyday a birthday, years turned centuries, every minute a rebirth and a moment a blessing.

the me who worships herself like the goddess she is
the one who praises the magician that they are
and the knight and shining armor
that he always was

The me who believes in the heaven above knowing fully
well that's where everything
came from

The me who clearly sees that
I am my own everything

And the me who understands entirely
the weight of saying

I love you.

thank you

Completed 13:31 2/26.

Made in the USA
Middletown, DE
08 March 2024

50550763R00031